Are You an
ANIMAL LOVER
or ABUSER ?

YOUR ANSWERS TO
3 QUESTIONS WILL SURPRISE YOU

MAGGIE CHEUNG

Table of Contents

PART I: From Corporate to Cat Poop | 1

Why I No Longer Drive a Mercedes | 3

I Thought I Was a BIG Animal Lover | 5

How It All Began | 7

Volunteering at the Cat Shelter | 9

I Found My Purpose | 15

The Abuse No One Knows About | 17

Are You an Animal Lover or Abuser? | 21

PART II: Your Answers to Three Questions

Will Surprise You | 23

Corporate Doesn't Want the Crazy Cat Lady | 25

Working with the Enemy | 27

Just Do It | 31

Dolphins! Dolphins! | 35

I Have a Company to Convince | 39

My Favorite Places to Visit Animals | 43

Question 1 | 49

Question 2 | 57

Question 3 | 65

PART III: I'm Confused! | 81

    Changing Lanes | 83

    I Thought It Was Beautiful | 85

    I Was an Animal Abuser | 87

    But Wait! All These Animal Places
        Are Animal Entertainment? | 89

PART IV: What Is the Solution? | 93

    Oh No… What Do I Do Now? | 95

    The One Exception | 99

    Rescue Is the Future. Sanctuary Is the Future | 103

    Dirty and Smelly Pigs | 105

    How Is an Animal Sanctuary Different from
        Animal Entertainment? | 109

    Real vs. Fake Animal Sanctuaries | 111

    Don't Shop! Please Adopt! | 129

    How to Cope with the Passing of Our Animals | 133

PART V: My Road | 138

    The Unfolding | 141

    To All the Animal Lovers | 143

    Keep Dreaming, Keep Chasing | 145

PART VI: Conclusion | 149

    Be Curious, Be Skeptical | 151

PART VII: Frequently Asked Questions | 153

    More Questions | 155

    But My Kids Love Zoos | 157

    I Wish I Could Just Eat and Sleep All Day! | 161

    What If Animals Could Have Both Luxury
        and Freedom? | 163

    Can't Animals Work Too? | 165

    Are the Fancy Horseback Riding Lessons
        Any Different? | 167

    Isn't Keeping Cats Indoors the Same as
        Life-Imprisonment? | 171

    Rescued Cat and Dog Cafés | 175

    How Can an Animal Sanctuary Survive? | 177

    Am I a Hypocrite for Supporting Farm Animal
        Sanctuaries While Also Eating Meat? | 179

About the Author | 183

Acknowledgments | 185

Notes | 189

Bibliography | 191

PART I

From Corporate to Cat Poop

Why I No Longer Drive a Mercedes

Sometimes, I still miss dressing in a fancy suit and heels, cruising in my elegant ride, and working on the top floors in the busiest downtowns. But I do not regret taking this wild turn for a single minute.

I would have just gone to work, made money, spent money, had fun, and then died. I would have lived a life where everything was about me — my career, my wealth, my family, and my happiness. I would have never stopped questioning why I existed on Earth.

Until one day, the most magical thing happened to me.

It was the moment that God scooped me up from the street where I had been wandering like a stray cat and set me on the path to a new purpose.

I Thought I Was a BIG Animal Lover

Like many of us, I have loved animals ever since I was a little kid. I grew up with kitties and puppies in my house, and I've had rabbits, hamsters, birds, and fish. I thought animals were all so cute; I loved seeing them, petting them, and hugging them. Whenever there was a chance to be around animals, whether it was at a zoo, aquarium, animal farm, animal café, horseback riding, swimming with dolphins, you name it, I would run for it. I've done it all and loved every minute of it.

All my life, I thought I was a big animal lover.

I had a terrible definition of "animal lover."

How It All Began

My name is Maggie Cheung, and I was born and raised in Hong Kong. After high school, I went to college in Boston, Massachusetts, in the United States. Back home, back then, choosing a major wasn't about chasing your dreams; it was more about being practical, particularly when it came to securing a job. Accounting seemed like a solid bet, especially because you could snag a professional license. Thus, after graduating with an accounting degree, I followed the expected career path of becoming a certified public accountant. I worked my butt off at one of the world's largest accounting firms. The hours and pressure were crazy, but it opened my wide eyes to the glamor of the corporate world. I hated my job, but I thought, *Hey, who actually likes their job? That's life.*

Years passed, and that kind of work lifestyle started to make me wonder why I existed. Eventually, I made up my mind. *Screw it, I'm out of here.*

I was really scared to leave the only career I'd known behind, but that didn't stop me as I packed my things.

I moved to the beautiful island of Jeju in South Korea, where I got married and started a new chapter. It was then that I remembered I always wanted to volunteer at an animal shelter but never had the time.

In 2016, I signed up to volunteer at a local, government-run shelter, and that's how it all began...

Volunteering at the Cat Shelter

It was a scorching summer day with temperatures over 95°F (35°C). When I opened the door of the cat shelter for the first time, the smell and the scene before my eyes shocked me. It was a broken-looking shack. The place was full of feces — in the cages, on the floor, on the wall. I couldn't tell if the bowls full of liquid were water, urine, or vomit. All the cats were meowing in distress, reaching out of their cages like zombies, desperate to get out as soon as they saw people. My heart sank. *Oh my, how could they live like this?* It was worse than euthanasia.

That day changed my life.

I wondered, *Who could be responsible for this atrocity?* The answer cut deep: we are.

Where did the shelter cats come from?

Each year, millions of kittens are bred by pet shops or born on the street, millions of cats are given up by their human parents, and millions are euthanized in shelters. The cycle keeps repeating.

Only then did I realize, I had contributed to this brutality in every way! When I was little, we kept cats and let them run in and out of the house at will. We didn't know anything about spaying and neutering. And you bet I loved visiting pet shops.

All my life I had thought I was a cat lover. It never occurred to me that my ignorance made me one of the very humans who created this worldwide disaster. And now, right in front of my eyes, it was coming back to bite me.

I dropped everything I was doing and began to volunteer at that shelter almost full-time. As I immersed myself in the work, I encountered all kinds of problems, from the never-ending cleaning duties to health issues like vomiting, diarrhea, ear mites, eye infections, and the deadly parvovirus. And then there were the catfights. It was heart-wrenching to keep them in cages, but if I let them out, they would try to kill each other.

I was consumed by the place. Because of the endless problems, my brain kept spinning for solutions. My mind was always preoccupied with the kitties. I saw them during the day, and I dreamt about them at night.

Interestingly, my previous job at one of the "Big Four" accounting firms paid well, paraded me around as a smart professional, and secured me a guaranteed future, but I could not have hated it more. Working at the shelter, I sweat a lot, got injured a lot, and cried a lot. This job did not pay me, and people thought I was stupid and had nothing better to do for me to be working there. This job hurt me and gave me no future. But guess what? I LOVED it.

Almost four years have passed since I first opened the door to that shack, and many things changed for the better. The place was cleaner, and the kitties looked more comfortable and healthier. We implemented a neutering program, which was one of the greatest improvements. I often dragged in abandoned furniture I found sitting outside, covered it with blankets, and added a few decorations to spruce up the place. The compliments and encouragement I received from others went a long way in easing the bitterness I had been carrying. Later the shack was torn down, and we were moved to a newly renovated place. I had always hated the cages. Eventually when our kitties got to have small, individual rooms of their own — even though each was just the size of a human toilet stall — I think I was even more excited than the cats.

I saw changes in each cat's life, but I started to wonder how I could change the system that created this suffering in the first place.

The cat shelter in summer of 2016,
a week into my volunteering there.

Six months into my volunteering at the shelter.

Two years into my volunteering at the shelter.

I Found My Purpose

I was sure that working with cats and other animals would be my lifelong career. Although I was reluctant to leave "my" kitties behind, I kept asking myself how many more kitties I could help, and how many more people I could influence, if I fought the problem and not just the symptoms. It felt meaningless to pick up litter every day if society was not educated to stop littering.

I had a strong feeling it was time for me to step out of the shelter. I recalled the ability and influence that I saw in the corporate world: the wealth of brilliant minds and the abundance of financial resources. I wondered if I could make the biggest difference by going back to that powerful place and using it to bring more help and benefits to animal welfare. And that's exactly what I decided to do!

The Abuse No One Knows About

Most people who consider themselves animal lovers still visit zoos, animal farms, and aquariums, unknowingly supporting an industry that actually causes suffering for millions of animals.

Most people know that factory farming is bad for animals. But almost no one knows the suffering caused by animal entertainment. In fact, animal entertainment is worse. Yes, you heard me right: using an animal for entertainment is worse than eating an animal.

Why?

When we eat an animal, at least we know we killed

it. But when we participate in animal entertainment, we still think we are ANIMAL LOVERS. That is scary!

Most of my own friends, including those involved in cat and dog rescues, participate in animal entertainment activities without realizing the damage. On social media, I often see friends taking their children to feed baby cows on farms, ride donkeys at the fair, and enjoy the company of meerkats on their laps at animal cafés.

I often feel sad, but I stay quiet. If I reach out to a friend and come across as preachy, soon enough I will be "that" person. You know, the big church friend who annoys the heck out of people because she tries to preach to every single person around her? Despite having this urge to speak out, I am extra cautious because the last thing I want to do is turn people away.

I have been searching for the right method and waiting for the right moment for years.

Finally, I have found a way to share this information in just three questions. After rejoining a corporate business, I used these three simple questions to convince the board of a $100-million-USD project, which will have over a million annual visitors, to pump the brakes on animal entertainment and switch lanes to animal welfare.

If these questions worked on the group of traditional Korean men running this corporation who originally didn't care about animal rights, I believe it will work on my own friends and you. Many of you animal lovers simply haven't thought about it before. All you need is a gentle nudge in the right direction.

This is the reason why I wrote this book.

Are You an Animal Lover or Abuser?

If you have purchased this book, you are most likely an "animal lover." Congratulations! In this book, I will ask you three simple questions. By the end, you will either see that you are a true animal lover or, if I have proven otherwise, I hope you will have gained a new understanding of what it really means to love animals and be inspired to make a difference.

PART II

YOUR ANSWERS TO THREE QUESTIONS WILL SURPRISE YOU

Corporate Doesn't Want
the Crazy Cat Lady

After I decided it was time to leave the shelter, I brushed up my resume and submitted it to a wealthy corporation in Jeju. At the time, they were looking for a Corporate Social Responsibility Director. Big corporations are always looking for ways to give back to society. I thought, *Alrighty, that's exactly what I want. I'm going to help you spend money well, but on ANIMALS!*

Everything in the interview went perfectly, and I felt confident I had already gotten the job. As I was leaving, they told me, "Why don't you prepare a very brief proposal on what project you might do if we were to have you on board?"

"Sure!" I said.

I thought, *You bet! I have a kick-ass concept on how to care for Jeju's stray cats. It would benefit both the community kitties and the neighborhood, and it's going to make your corporation a favorite among animal supporters!*

I was on fire.

Then a friend cautioned me, "Maggie, if you show them this proposal, you might not get the job."

I felt like a bucket of ice water had suddenly been poured over my head. But my friend was right. I didn't realize I had gotten carried away. It was a risky move. They would either love the idea or think I was crazy. I could have played it safe and presented something more conventional that any corporation would like and bought my way into the company first, but I had a strong belief in my idea. My feelings towards stray cats were so intense that I didn't want to hide them, so I took the risk.

And, of course, my grand idea crashed and burned. I didn't get the job.

Working with the Enemy

Life is interesting, though. When God closes one door, He opens another. Just when I was all excited about the social responsibility job, my husband, Ben, came home and asked me to go to dinner with some of his business acquaintances.

Me: "Who are they?"

Ben: "One of them is the man who is building the safari theme park in Jeju."

Me: "Are you kidding me? Safari? The zoo? We are protesting it. We are technically enemies. I'm not going."

But immediately after, my mind started spinning: *Wait, don't be a loser. Aren't you always telling yourself how small you are and how little you can do for the animals? This man is building a safari. He is a person who can affect millions of others. Just go to the dinner and see what happens.*

South Korea is a much more traditional society than I was used to in the United States or Hong Kong. I was never an outspoken person and, on top of that, my Korean is equivalent to an elementary schooler's. Even though I had a gazillion questions I wanted to ask this man, I stayed quiet through most of dinner, trying not to act foolish or inappropriate.

That night, I couldn't sleep. *Mag, you are pathetic. You have so much passion and faith in what you do. You have to tell this person your idea.* The next day, I asked Ben to arrange another lunch with him. By a twist of fate, it happened to be on the same day and at the same place as my other job interview.

That afternoon, the man told me the safari part of the park was scrapped. People protested against it, and the government wouldn't grant a permit. He was actually changing the whole project to a forest nature park. No safari? I was smiling in my heart. I shared with him my thoughts about how the safari wouldn't have been able to sustain itself in the long run and how businesses could treat and handle animals ethically in the future.

A week later, I received the news that I didn't get the other position. But the very next day, the man called and said, "Come work for me."

Just Do It

I had absolutely no experience on how to build a theme park.

What am I going to do in this company?

What will happen next?

I didn't even speak much Korean, for Christ's sake.

Whenever I got stuck, I always turned to a very dear friend, a smart and intelligent man whom I consider my mentor.

He said to me, "It's a no-brainer, Maggie, just GO! You'll be fine. You'll regret it if this park ends up doing anything bad to whatever animals they may have later."

He made the choice so easy for me.

So far, this was all I knew about the project:

- Almost everyone in the company was traditional, Korean, male, and over 50 years old.

- The safari part of the plan had been turned down by the government, and the company was now planning to build a forest nature park.

- The park would cover almost a million square meters (250 acres) of land in the woods.

- The budget was at least $100 million USD.

- It expected to attract over a million visitors annually.

- Just like many other tourist spots in Jeju, animals will be brought in to attract and entertain visitors.

At that time, I realized I had two options:

1. Stand OUTSIDE the park to protest against animal entertainment AFTER it's built, or

2. Get INSIDE the company now to change it BEFORE the park is built.

I picked option two and concluded that I only had one mission:

I was determined to make things right for the animals.

How?

No idea. I would figure it out.

Meanwhile, ever since I came to Korea, my life had been a roller coaster, and I'd actually gotten used to riding it without being able to see what was in front of me.

Just like that, I started working for the company without any discussion of salary or benefits or anything at all. In fact, I wasn't sure if I would even get paid. But hey, I worked for the shelter for four years for free. I had nothing to lose.

Dolphins! Dolphins!

After volunteering at the cat shelter, my definition of love for animals changed. I used to love them just because they were cute and they made me happy, but what is love actually? Had I ever done anything to benefit them?

Not at all.

I started to think something was wrong with the places I used to love: zoos, animal farms, horseback riding ranches, animal cafés, aquariums, water parks where you could swim with dolphins.

Growing up in Hong Kong surrounded by high-rises, all the animals I encountered were in zoos or pet shops. Except for wild birds and mice, I don't remember ever seeing an animal in "nature."

When I first moved to Jeju Island, I traded the

concrete jungle for an endless stretch of beautiful ocean. I had heard that dolphins graced these waters, but spotting them required some luck. So, my eyes were always looking for dolphins.

One gorgeous day we were driving along the coast, every inch of the peaceful ocean sparkling under the sun. All of a sudden, my husband called out in Korean, "Dolphins! Dolphins!" My eyes immediately started scanning the waves from left to right. There they were! One fin, two fins... My heart raced. It was a whole pod of them! My jaw dropped as I watched their graceful bodies arching and leaping above the water's surface. When I saw them doing a spin and flip, I screamed mutely as I feared the slightest noise might scare them away.

This amazing encounter lasted less than a minute, but the memory will stay with me for a lifetime. The scene before me was one of complete calm and peace. At the same time, it was a powerful awakening that struck my heart. As I was watching these magnificent creatures free-riding the waves, my inner voice whispered, *I'm so sorry.* Memories of dolphin tank shows and swimming with dolphins flashed before me, experiences I once labeled as "awesome."

In twelve years of living in Jeju, I have only seen dolphins twice.

Now I silently wish to them: *swim far away, live free, and never get caught by humans.*

I Have a Company
to Convince

Seeing for my own eyes how much it cost the dolphins to go from the wild to captivity was life changing. But most people never get to have this magical experience, so how can they learn about the damages of animal entertainment?

Here are some typical arguments against the industry:

"It is selfish. Businesses are using animals to entertain us and to make money."

"There is nothing cute about confining animals to unnatural environments, subjecting them to constant handling, and exploiting them for profit."

"If you truly love animals, you should not take

advantage of them. You should not take away their freedom."

"Animals belong to nature, not to us. Humans have no right over them. Leave them alone!"

Blah blah blah...

These are all true statements, but come on, people just don't want to hear them. They are not convincing. I knew I would not even be able to persuade my own friends with arguments like this, not to mention an older-generation company.

I was stumped.

Until one day...

Quite reluctantly, I had to interview the owners of an animal farm.

Life is full of surprises. That day, when I left that animal farm, I had hit the jackpot! I found my perfect answer on how to convince my company and offered them a proposal they could not reject.

**Animal lovers, are you ready to find out
if you are an animal abuser?**

My Favorite Places
to Visit Animals

The set of questions I came up with convinced these conservative Korean businessmen to shift the course of this substantial corporate investment venture. Before I tell you about the changes, I want to walk through this same set of questions with you.

If you or your children love animals, there must be places where you enjoy seeing or interacting with the animals. Think of three of your favorite places, and write them down below.

If you have an e-book, simply grab a piece of paper and write down your answers. This exercise will have the most impact if you write your answers down rather than just keep them in your mind. Your answers will surprise you, just like the board members were surprised by theirs.

	My favorite places to visit animals:
1	
2	
3	

Meanwhile, I'll go through this exercise and share my own answers.

My favorite places I used to love visiting animals:

1. Animal farms

2. Animal cafés

3. Horseback riding ranches

Now, I'm going to ask you three questions.

QUESTION 1

WHERE ARE THE ANIMALS FROM?

Don't rush. Take your time to think about where the animal you see at each location might have come from. You don't need to research the most accurate answer; it's fine to make a guess.

QUESTION 1

	My favorite places to visit animals	Where are the animals from?
1		
2		
3		

Again, I will walk through the exercise along with you, making simple, logical guesses for my own locations.

1. Animal farms

Question 1: Where are the animals from?

Answer:

Among goats, sheep, cows, and more, it's common to encounter the adorable sight of baby animals on animal farms. Take baby cows, for instance; where do they come from?

Baby cows must come from mother cows, right?

However, I have never wondered how the mother cows get pregnant. Do they get pregnant naturally? Do they mate with male cows?

I'll do a quick search on Google: "How do cows get pregnant on farms?"

Whoa! It's like opening a can of worms. There is a lot of disturbing information about the milk industry out there. But for now, I'll stay focused and find the answer to my question. It seems that the answer is artificial insemination.

Okay, mother cows are usually artificially inseminated to give birth to a calf.[1]

2. Animal cafés

Question 1: Where are the animals from?

Answer:

There are various types of animal cafés, from raccoon and owl cafés to ones with meerkats and kangaroos. These wild animals, I would assume, would normally be living in their natural habitats, such as forests or remote grasslands.

So, how did they find themselves in these cafés?

Again, keep in mind you don't have to do a lot of detailed research. I'm just here to take you through the thought process.

It's likely that the café owners acquired these wild and exotic animals by purchasing them from somewhere or even importing them from other countries.

In essence, the answer to this question is that these animals in cafés were probably captured from the wild, bred in captivity, or traded in various ways.

3. Horseback riding ranches

Question 1: Where are the animals from?

Answer:

Some of the horses are retired from horse racing, while others have been bred and raised on horse farms.

Just take your best guesses. Don't overthink it.
Now, let's move on to the next question.

QUESTION 2

WHY ARE THE ANIMALS HERE?

The second question is not difficult, and the answer is quite obvious. But please do me a favor and keep writing down your answers. I will continue with my examples.

QUESTION 2

	My favorite places to visit animals	Why are the animals here?
1		
2		
3		

1. Animal farms

Question 2: Why are the animals here?

Answer:

The presence of baby cows allows me to purchase a bottle of milk and feed them. They are here to entertain people.

Now this has made me think: *Why am I the one feeding these calves with a bottle? Where are their mothers?*

The truth is, these baby cows are intentionally separated from their mothers. This separation occurs because their mothers' milk is used for human consumption, for our children, and so that I can bottle-feed these calves for my amusement.

2. Animal cafés

Question 2: Why are the animals here?

Answer:

The animals are in the café so that I can pet them, play with them, and take pictures with them. They make me happy and smile!

They are also here to entertain people.

3. Horseback riding ranches

Question 2: Why are the animals here?

Answer:

Obviously, the horses are here for me to ride, but I don't see any problem with that.

Their bodies are so big and strong. It's an elegant sport, and the horses are treated very well.

Okay, okay, I get it! The answer to this question is...

The horses are here for people's pleasure and entertainment.

If you feel yourself becoming agitated or defensive at any point, please close the book and take a break. Come back tomorrow. Turning you away is the last thing I want. I know this can be awkward or even boring, but if an entire room of Korean business leaders and professionals changed their minds because of this exercise, I hope you'll give it a chance.

The last question…

QUESTION 3

WHERE WILL THE ANIMALS GO?

All of these animals are beautiful and healthy when we see them, but eventually, they will grow old, get sick, and will no longer be able to fulfill their role of entertaining people. When that time comes, where will they go?

When faced with this question for the first time, I realized I had never thought about it in my entire life, but the answer was not difficult to guess.

We are almost there. I know you might have already reached my conclusion, but it's important to finish this exercise with me.

QUESTION 3

	My favorite places to visit animals	Where will the animals go?
1		
2		
3		

1. Animal farms

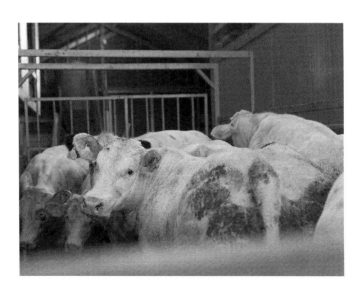

Question 3: Where will the animals go?

Answer:

Baby cows cannot remain calves forever. In fact, they grow fast.

When the baby cows grow up, they must go somewhere. You might have never thought about this, but can you guess where they go? To the slaughterhouse.[2]

Mother cows are artificially inseminated to keep giving birth to baby cows so that we can keep taking pictures with them and feeding them from bottles. When they are no longer babies, they are loaded onto a truck and sent to the slaughterhouse for meat.

I used to visit animal farms where they don't have baby animals, just adult cattle, goats, and sheep grazing in pastures. As a visitor, I didn't feed them, pet them, or interrupt their lives at all. I simply enjoyed the peaceful scenery. In this case, the animals might have a less stressful life, but in the end, they still go to the same place. The slaughterhouse.

2. Animal cafés

Question 3: Where will the animals go?

Answer:

Animal cafés have emerged as a prominent tourist attraction in South Korea and various other Asian countries. Initially themed around cats or dogs, these cafés have since expanded to include a variety of wild and exotic animals.

How many animal cafés can last twenty years or even ten years? In cities where businesses face rapid turnover and closures, postings that read, "Urgent Adoption Needed! Business Closing!" have become a common sight.

Where do you think the animals will go if the café is no longer profitable? What are the chances that the café owner will take them all home and they will live happily ever after?

If the animals are cats or dogs, the café owner may call shelters or let other kind souls take care of their mess. If the animals are wild, they may be sold to another animal entertainment venue. And if they are edible, they may be sold as meat.[3]

3. Horseback riding ranches

Question 3: Where will the animals go?

Answer:

What happens to the horses when they become old and are no longer fit for riding? Taking care of horses is very expensive, and if a horseback riding ranch's purpose is to provide pleasure and entertainment to people, the horse is useless once he loses his ability to generate profit for the ranch.

In Korea, the majority of horses in the animal entertainment industry are sent to slaughterhouses.[4] A horse trainer told me that if the horses are too old and their meat gets too tough to eat, they may be ground into horse bone powder, a medicinal souvenir that Jeju is famous for.

Photo Credit: PETA

I know many of you are horse lovers, experts, or even horse whisperers. Some of you might have spent a substantial amount of money for your children to learn to ride horses or pursue equine studies in college. You must be starting to feel uncomfortable and maybe a little annoyed with me.

I know exactly how you feel because that is how I felt! And believe me, it's an uncomfortable feeling.

That's why I give special attention to horseback riding in the FAQ section at the end of the book.

I have now asked you my three questions. They were very simple, right? Here is a summary of my answers.

	Question 1	Question 2	Question 3
My favorite places to visit animals	WHERE are the animals from?	WHY are the animals here?	WHERE will the animals go?
1. Animal farms	Artificial insemination	To entertain people	Slaughterhouse
2. Animal cafés	Captured / bred	To entertain people	Sold to other businesses / euthanasia
3. Horseback riding ranches	Bred (artificial insemination)	To entertain people	Slaughterhouse / euthanasia

What about you? What are your answers?

	Question 1	Question 2	Question 3
My favorite places to visit animals	WHERE are the animals from?	WHY are the animals here?	WHERE will the animals go?
1.			
2.			
3.			

After you see how animals are harmed by these "happy" places you love visiting, do you still think you are an animal lover?

PART III

I'm Confused!

Changing Lanes

That day, with a list of questions in hand, I headed off with little expectation to interview the owners of an animal farm. As I left the farm, something extraordinary happened.

It was as if all the questions I had prepared were swirling together in a deep pool of thoughts. But then, like buoys in the water, these three questions and the answers I had received bobbed to the surface, breaking through the stillness of my mind like something coming up for air. In that instant, it became undeniably clear: *It's that simple!*

I couldn't wait to organize my thoughts that night. The next morning, I walked into my boss' office with a single sheet of A4 paper, containing fewer than 100 words I had translated into Korean. Back then, I spoke far less Korean than I do now, but I didn't need sophisticated negotiation skills. This straightforward truth could speak for itself, loud and clear.

I've always believed that we aren't just paid to point out problems, our value is in identifying the problem AND providing a solution. That day, I didn't just explain the issue of animal entertainment, I offered my boss the solution.

He gazed at the paper for a while. Then his face broke into a smile, "Very good."

I couldn't hide my own smile as I continued, "We are a corporation, a leader in society. For both human consciousness or corporate strategy, our path forward is obvious."

Later, I made a formal presentation to the company. It marked the moment when I was able to steer the whole company to change lanes from animal harm to animal support, and they gave me the green light to proceed with the solution.

I Thought It
Was Beautiful

I have done a lot of self-reflection on the places I used to LOVE, feel proud of venturing, brag about visiting, and where I have taken so many pictures.

One vivid memory takes me back to a fair where we were surrounded by baby goats. Children were running around, giggling, and having fun. It was a beautiful day, wonderful weather, innocent kids, and cute baby animals. I loved it. The little goats were so adorable, I couldn't resist picking one up and holding her in my arms while my family cheered and snapped a few photos. I had such a good time.

Now, I feel like a ghost standing at the crime scene, watching the replay.

Gosh, the goats were just babies. All they wanted was their moms, and instead they were chased around by countless screaming kids all day long. I saw a little girl, trying to grab a baby goat and hold him in her arms, but the goat kept slipping away and running off. The little girl kept chasing, and whenever she was able to grab the goat and lift him in the air, her mother would cheer, "Baby, look this way, this way!" Taking the most precious pictures.

That little girl was me.

Only now am I seeing the truth. Even if the goats weren't slaughtered eventually, I wonder what kind of life that is, being grabbed and pulled, trying to escape, and being caught again. This kind of stress, day in and day out, every day, is just too much for these innocent animals to bear.

This is animal abuse.

And I did it while laughing.

What's worse is that I believed it's an act of "LOVE."

I even called myself an "animal lover."

I once thought it was a beautiful scene, but the truth behind this picture is kids tormenting and exhausting helpless baby goats.

What a sad reality!

I Was an
Animal Abuser

Early in this book, when I first brought up "animal entertainment," you may have found yourself wondering, "What exactly does that mean?" You're not alone; many others share this same curiosity. The term "animal entertainment" has received far less attention than it rightfully deserves.

Here's the simple definition:

Animal entertainment is an industry by which animals are taken away from their natural habitats to entertain people and often suffer or are killed in the process.

Since I was a child, I have loved animals. Simply out of instinct, I called myself an animal lover, but what I really loved was having animals to entertain me. All of my animal loving was supporting animal entertainment. Everything I had done was hurting the animals.

Damn.

Animal lover? Nowhere near it, I was an animal abuser.

But Wait!
All These Places Are
Animal Entertainment?

J ust like me, you might be shaking your head in confusion around now.

"But I've loved these places all my life. Animal farms, animal cafés, donkey rides at the fair, alpaca farms, horse carriages in the park, horseback riding ranches, zoos, and aquariums..." The list goes on and on. We have incredibly fond memories of visiting these places, and they've made up a significant part of our childhood.

However, the shocking truth is many places where you interact with animals are animal entertainment businesses. (Except for one place, which I will get to later).

I know it's hard to accept, and you might be in denial. I was.

The animal entertainment industry has used and twisted our love for animals. Children have been misled all their lives. We thought we loved animals, but we did not realize our happiness was built on the sacrifice of their freedom. We have been supporting these businesses only to harm the animals.

Yes, the animal entertainment industry is fully responsible for it, and you are also the victim. Yet, these businesses exist all over the world, and they are not going to disappear overnight. So now, it's your decision to make. If you want to fix it and make a positive change, it's time to rewrite your definition of what it means to be an animal lover. True animal lovers should do good for the animals and not contribute to their harm.

I know it's very hard to quit, but this will be a life-changing moment. Think of it like overcoming an addiction. At first, we see the substance as magic, and we get caught up in its joys. Even when we realize it's evil, breaking free is a painful challenge.

But you can do it! Your children can do it! It may not happen overnight, so give yourself some time.

I have faith in you because I know you are a true
animal lover!

PART IV

WHAT IS THE SOLUTION?

Oh No... What Do
I Do Now?

U p to this point, even if you agree and you understand, changing our actions can be hard because we all get excited to see animals. To tell ourselves that every place we've visited has involved animal entertainment and that we should stop going is just too hard! I hear you.

I remember when I first learned about the dark side of zoos, circuses, and elephant rides. It was heartbreaking to learn how the animals were captured from the wild and tortured by stressful and cruel training. Animal activists urged the world to stop supporting the animal entertainment business, and my first reaction was, "I agree, I understand, and I shouldn't be supporting this evil industry." But man, it stinks! Because all of a sudden I lost all these activities that I did for fun.

People are afraid and reluctant to lose things, and that's why some get defensive and resist. "Please don't tell me that, I don't want to know about it," they say.

In the beginning, I meant to do the right thing, so I stopped going to zoos, but I was forcing myself, and I still thought it sucked. Then came a day when, for personal reasons, I found myself stepping into a zoo once more. Something changed.

For the first time, I saw the animals through different eyes. It hit me: those animals were not happy. The monkeys were miserable, begging for food, while all the children and adults stood by and laughed. My heart ached.

I no longer have to force myself to ditch the zoos because I was told it was the right thing to do. I feel it myself, and I feel for the animals.

Knowing something is 100% right doesn't mean I can easily do the right thing.

Knowing something is 100% wrong doesn't mean I can immediately quit doing the wrong thing.

Change has to come from within. We need TIME.

Give yourself time to adjust. Even go to the zoo again, see with a different perspective, and then make the right change.

If we force our children to stop going to zoos and playing with animals, they will cry. How about we teach them to put their hearts with the animals, open their eyes, and see again?

What Is the Solution Then?

The One Exception

So, let's take a step back and recap a little. Whenever I am planning to visit a place with animals, I ask myself three questions:

(1) Where are the animals from?

(2) Why are they here?

(3) Where will they go?

Sadly, the answers often lead to the conclusion that these places are pretty much animal entertainment businesses. This raises the question: If we want to avoid supporting the animal entertainment industry, does that mean we can only watch animals on the Discovery Channel? Does that mean I will never see real animals again?

The good news is, there is ONE EXCEPTION. There is one type of place that is FOR the animals and deserves our support.

Can you guess what it is?

The answer is an **animal sanctuary**.

Rescue Is the Future.
Sanctuary Is the Future.

I f you live in the US, even if you don't have much interest in animals, you are probably familiar with an animal sanctuary. However, in many Asian countries, including my home countries of Hong Kong and Korea, "animal sanctuary" is a term most people have not heard of.

So, what exactly is an animal sanctuary?

An animal sanctuary is a facility where animals are rescued and given quality care, protection, love, and respect for the rest of their lives.

There are different types of sanctuaries, such as companion animal sanctuaries, wildlife sanctuaries, exotic animal sanctuaries, and farm animal sanctuaries. For example, there are elephant sanctuaries in Thailand, bear sanctuaries in Vietnam, lion sanctuaries in Africa, and farm animal sanctuaries in the US and Australia.

Now, why do I say an animal sanctuary is the only exception that deserves our support?

Let's ask the three big questions again:

(1) Where are the animals from?

ALL animals at an animal sanctuary are rescued animals.

(2) Why are the animals here?

They are here simply to be protected, to live stress-free lives, and to educate people on how to love and respect animals properly.

(3) Where will the animals go?

Nowhere. The animals will live at the sanctuary with quality care and love until the end of their lives.

Rescue is the future. Sanctuary is the future.

Dirty and Smelly Pigs

Those years when I worked at the cat shelter were times of heavy labor and tough physical work. Each evening, upon returning home and finally finding a moment to sit down, my legs would just give in, and I could barely get back up. I thought that working with farm animals ten to a hundred times larger than cats was going to break my back. Regardless, my excitement was uncontainable when I had the chance to intern at a farm sanctuary.

After thirty hours in transit and multiple plane rides to the other side of the world, I arrived at the sanctuary located atop a breathtaking mountain.

Among cows, sheep, goats, and chickens, the sanctuary housed over 100 pigs, which were our primary responsibility. Our day started with the first feeding at 6:30 in the morning. Each animal had its own dietary formula according to their health condition, specifying the precise amount of main feed, fruits, vitamins, and supplements they got. Their meal times were scheduled throughout the day, and the sanctuary made sure that the weaker animals received special care, including separate feedings and additional meals.

I was handed three bowls of special meals to give to Posie, Chatty, and Theo.

Having arrived at the sanctuary only two days prior, I got nervous. "I can't remember which ones they are..."

A fellow volunteer offered a reassuring smile. "Don't worry. They know!"

As I headed towards the paddock, a warm smile emerged within me. I was greeted by the cutest sight: three piggies with wagging tails were waiting excitedly at the gate.

After meals, the piggies roamed freely all over the mountain. You would be amazed at how far they wandered. I was watching the junior pigs from a distance. They were playful and naughty, chasing each other around like little kids. The moment one of them spotted me, the little gang all raced forward, wrapping me in their adorable chaos, and turning me into a ball of laughter.

If I had not worked in the sanctuary, I would never have believed that the pigs' paddock was the cleanest! They don't pee or poop where they eat or sleep. It was so healing to watch them make their beds. The refreshing scent of the clean, dry straw filled the air of the paddock. Their comfy expressions, nestled within the golden, fluffy bedding, made me feel as if I was watching a mattress commercial.

It made me wonder, *But pigs have the reputation of being dirty and smelly...* We have always heard, "Pigs are disgusting, they eat their own crap!"

Then I realized the problem.

Ah... It was the living conditions that were dirty and smelly. All the pigs had to eat, pee, and poop in the same cramped, stinky space. But who is responsible for this?

I sighed. *We have been blaming it on the pigs.*

Once again, it was an eye-opening moment when I realized I had been wrong about this the whole time.

I had never been this close to a pig before; the nearest I had come was having one on my dinner plate. I must confess, I didn't have much interest in pigs because I didn't think they were very cute. Also, I was one of those people who thought they were dirty and smelly. Yet, the sanctuary opened my eyes and brought justice to the piggies. I could almost hear them: "Don't you see? I am smart, affectionate, and I like to be clean too!"

How Is an
Animal Sanctuary
Different from
Animal Entertainment?

Rescue is the future. Sanctuary is the future.

With this said, it's not hard to imagine that smart business owners would immediately change their brand to "animal sanctuary" but operate no differently than animal entertainment.

An animal sanctuary may have animals, visitors, and charge an entrance fee, so how can we differentiate a genuine sanctuary from a fake one?

Before diving into the answers, I must warn you: this chapter is going to be boring, and I am at risk of losing your attention. I am trying my best to keep it short and to the point, however, I want you to understand that this is an extremely important chapter because the last thing I want is for you to walk into a FAKE sanctuary!

Real vs. Fake
Animal Sanctuaries

A true animal sanctuary must have ALL of the following characteristics. Animal entertainment will have only SOME. Remember, it is not a pick-and-choose situation. These are common-sense needs. So, observe the animals, be curious, and ask questions.

A real animal sanctuary must have:

1. Rescued animals only.

2. Spacious living environments.

3. Clean and hygienic barns.

4. Animals that are treated as individuals and not commodities.

5. Monitoring for the health condition of each animal.

6. Stress-free environments.

7. Spaying and neutering (extremely important).

8. Life-long quality care.

9. A mission that is for the animals, not for the benefit of people.

Real vs. Fake
Animal Sanctuaries

1. Rescued animals only

In animal entertainment, animals are often purchased, traded, or bred to attract visitors.

In an animal sanctuary, all animals are rescued. These animals may include a male calf not wanted by the dairy industry, a half-dead chicken that was tossed out with the farm garbage, a pig that fell off the truck on the way to the slaughterhouse, an old donkey retiring from pulling a tourist carriage, or a baby tiger used as a photo prop for tourists.

2. Spacious living environments

In animal entertainment establishments, animals are often kept in small and insufficient living spaces.

I remember visiting an aquarium as a kid where there was a giant, glass tank custom-built for a beaver. He was swimming at high speed, shooting from one side of the tank, through the tunnels, over my head, to the other side, again and again. I stood there watching him for a very long time. I thought that the whole set-up looked very expensive, but the beaver must have been bored to death repeating this pattern forever.

Even though well-funded zoos and aquariums spend so much money on the animals, it's just a luxury prison. The animals can never get the space and freedom they need.

Why?

So that we, the visitors, can see the animals up close.

On the other hand, an animal sanctuary might not have an obscene amount of money to build an extravagant home for the rescued animals. Rather, they are located in real natural areas to provide animals sufficient space to roam freely.

If an animal feels like wandering far away on a particular day and the visitor doesn't get to meet them, you are out of luck. A real sanctuary would not force animals to interact with visitors by confining them. Because a sanctuary is for the animals, not for the benefit of people.

3. Clean and hygienic barns

At some farms, we see animals peacefully grazing in spacious pastures during the day. However, at night, they are crammed in dirty barns, lying in their own urine and feces. If you pay closer attention to the animals themselves, you'll notice that their fur is dull and matted with dried dung.

In real animal sanctuaries, you would be amazed at how much work and effort is put in to maintain a clean and hygienic barn. The barns are lined with dry, fresh straw that is frequently replaced, ensuring that the animals' living space is comfortable and sanitary. The animals' fur is clean and shiny. Like human kids, animals like to play and roll in the mud. However, no animal would choose to eat and sleep in their own poop every day.

Tourists are often presented with this beautiful scene (above) while the cows actually live like this (below).

Poor living conditions in the cow barn

Hygienic and well-managed horse barn

4. Animals that are treated as individuals and not commodities

Imagine you're planning to have children. A responsible parent would consider if they have the ability to raise and provide proper care for each child first. An animal sanctuary works in the same way.

A sanctuary treats animals as individuals and takes on the responsibility of providing them with the care they need. The staff knows each animal's background, personality, health condition, likes and dislikes. The caregivers also know which animals are good buddies with each other, which animals don't get along, and which need to be kept separate to avoid fights.

As a result, animal sanctuaries carefully evaluate if they have the capability, space, manpower, and money to rescue an animal because they take full responsibility for providing not just care but good care. Unlike a human child who will grow up and become independent someday, rescued animals will need to live under the care of the sanctuary for the rest of their lives.

On the other hand, animals in entertainment operations are often treated as commodities or "things." That's why in petting zoos or animal farms, we can easily find dozens or even hundreds of sheep, goats, and cows crowded together in one facility. I've seen male goats fighting with their horns because they are locked in the same enclosure. I've also noticed fresh, open wounds and other scars on animals. Imagine that kind of stress.

Animal farm owners mostly just care about removing the feces, because if the place stinks, visitors won't like it and won't return. They don't plan well, and so they don't care well.

5. Monitoring for the health condition of each animal

When I volunteered at the cat shelter, I had no prior experience, and no one was there to teach me. But when you truly care, the next steps become common sense, and you just figure them out. Despite having over 100 cats sometimes, I knew each one's eating habits and health condition — who eats more, who likes which kind of food, who suddenly didn't eat that morning, who ate too much and threw up, who has diarrhea — because I deeply cared about their health.

It's important to know that not all animals in an animal sanctuary will be in perfect health. In reality, animals can get sick, and some of them may have been rescued precisely because they have a serious illness. However, what truly matters is the sanctuary's dedication to providing comprehensive care for every animal. If you were to inquire about any animal's health, the sanctuary staff should be able to share specifics about their condition and the ongoing efforts to manage their sickness.

6. Stress-free environments

Animal entertainment businesses value how much fun the audience is having over how much stress the animal is experiencing.

At animal farms, being surrounded by children and adult visitors all day is very stressful for the animals. Some places even make the animals do tricks to make visitors giggle. In this island where I live, there are "shows" where pigs have been trained to slide down slopes to amuse and entertain visitors. Children and parents, while cheering and laughing at the performance, hardly realize the stress and discomfort experienced by these animals.

In an animal sanctuary, the goal is to educate the public on the proper way to care for, love, and respect animals. So, the well-being of the animals is always the first priority. Therefore, any public-facing programs are carefully designed, with each of the animal's unique personality taken into consideration, to ensure they do not cause any stress to the animals.

As a result, animal sanctuaries will always offer a guided tour with educational information, as opposed to allowing unaccompanied children to run and scream around the animals as they do at animal farms.

7. Spaying and neutering

I didn't truly understand the importance of spaying and neutering until I started to get personally involved in rescuing animals myself. I have to say, this is the MOST important part. It literally takes sweat, tears, and sometimes blood to rescue just one animal. What's even more challenging is the responsibility to take care of them for the rest of their lives.

There are countless animals out there that need rescuing. Rescuers and animal sanctuaries constantly wish they could afford one extra space to take in one more animal in need. In contrast, animal entertainers purposely breed their animals or let them become pregnant.

As a result, one fundamental distinction between a sanctuary and an animal entertainment facility is their approach to animal breeding. While animal entertainment facilities engage in continuous breeding and trading practices, a genuine sanctuary operates with a strong spaying and neutering program in place for all of its animals. The only exception is if the animal is already pregnant upon rescue.

So, if a place consistently promotes the presence of newborn animals, you know it's not an animal sanctuary!

8. Life-long quality care

As mentioned earlier, an old, sick, or handicapped animal is not going to make visitors happy. Their fate is most likely to be slaughtered or euthanized. On the other hand, once the animals are rescued by an animal sanctuary, they will live their entire lives with quality care, respect, and love.

However, there are conditions where euthanasia might happen in animal sanctuaries too. If an animal is very ill with a terminal condition and is in a lot of pain, then the sanctuary and their vet might choose euthanasia to spare the animal from prolonged suffering. This is a stark contrast to the entertainment industry that will put down not only old but healthy animals, and even young male calves, if they are not seen as profitable.

9. A mission that is for the animals, not for the benefit of people

Animal entertainment exploits animals, and it also exploits you. They use your love and your children's love for animals and turn it into something very unloving. We are misled into believing that we are animal lovers when, in reality, we are unknowingly funding their harm.

In contrast, animal sanctuaries are on a mission to educate the public. Why? Because they want to teach people so that more of us can support the protection of animals. In the end, education benefits the animals the most.

Farm Sanctuary SA, South Africa

Farm Sanctuary SA, South Africa

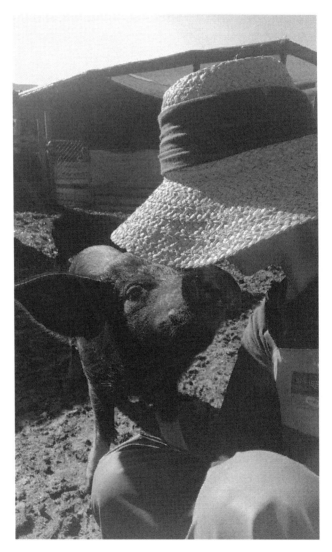

Greyton Farm Animal Sanctuary, South Africa

Your Home Can Be a Sanctuary Too!

Don't Shop!
Please Adopt!

I no longer use the word "pet," because I believe this concept is at the root of today's animal tragedy. The idea to "keep animals for our pleasure" is toxic.

Although the history of how humans evolved our relationship with cats and dogs is long and complex, the domestication of these animals is irreversible. Now imagine what would happen if people went further and tried to make wild exotic animals into pets simply because having one seems like a cool hobby, what would happen to them then?

Cats and dogs, as well as wild and exotic animals sold in pet shops, are no different from animals used for entertainment. If we acquire an animal through breeding or trading; if the primary reason we want an animal is for our pleasure, if later we give up this animal because he brings us more inconvenience than joy, guess what — we are engaging in animal entertainment for ourselves too.

To fix this, again, rescue is the solution.

Just like sanctuaries save animals that already need a home, rather than encouraging businesses to create more pets, we can help fix the problem — give a helping hand to rescuers and adopt rescued cats, dogs and other animals in need. Your home can be a sanctuary too!

Now I encourage you to take a moment and rethink. Ask yourself why you want an animal.

Then, hit the reset button on your mindset: try to switch from the "*me*" *mindset* to the "***them***" *mindset.*

What do I mean?

When I adopted my first pair of kitties (they were brother and sister), I was no saint myself. It was all about me wanting them simply because cats are cute, that's all. It was all about *me*.

The rescuer would tell me all the time how close the kitties were to death when she found them, how she did not give up on them, how they eventually pulled through, and how thankful she was that I adopted them together so they wouldn't have to be separated.

I really appreciated and respected the rescuer, but, to be honest, I couldn't feel what she felt. It wasn't until years later when I started volunteering at the shelter that I could finally feel every single bit of her effort. I felt the physical and emotional intensity. It was as if I could literally feel her heartbeat.

You may understand every word of my writing in this book, but if you want to truly feel it for yourself, I highly encourage you to get involved in rescues, be a volunteer, become a foster parent, or help in any way you can.

When you rescue, you'll naturally experience a switch in focus from "*me*" to "*them.*"

Then, you might find yourself wanting to adopt a rescued pup not because he's cute (in fact, he might look like a mess), but because he's hungry and skinny. It's about *them*.

Later, you won't abandon this pup when he turns into this chaotic rascal messing up your home and chewing on your socks and furniture. Instead, you might catch yourself smiling at the memory of his poor face, too scared to even make eye contact with you when you first brought him home. It's about **them**.

If you have made it to this point, I congratulate you because you have moved beyond the concept of having a "pet." I now encourage you to adopt the terms "companion animal" or "furry friend" and spread this other-centric mindset.

However, if you have never thought about it and find yourself accidentally running an animal entertainment, don't be too harsh on yourself; from now on, you are totally capable of turning your home into a sanctuary!

In life, when you learn to switch your focus from "*me*" to "*them*" — other people, other animals — you'll be amazed at how it can change your life. You'll get back way more than you give.

How to Cope with the Passing of Our Animals

When it comes to adoption, there is one concern I hear the most:

"I had a dog in the past. He was my family. It has been years since he died, but my heart is still broken. Every time I think about him, I still cry. I can't bring myself to have another companion animal because I just cannot bear the thought of going through their passing again."

Here is my response:

My kitties' rescuer taught me this. If we were to divide the world of people in terms of whether they like animals or not, there would be three types of people: (1) people who love animals, (2) people who do not like animals, and (3) people who neither love nor hate animals.

Out of these three types of people, type three, those who neither love nor hate animals, is the largest group.

Out of the three types of people, only type one, animal lovers, would consider having companion animals. They are the only ones who would adopt animals and support animal rescues. Despite surveys and statistics each year showing how the number of animal lovers and the number of households that have companion animals is on the rise, when compared to the total of the other two groups, this population is still the smallest.

So, when a person tells me in tears she cannot have another animal again because she cannot handle the pain of the animal eventually passing away, I would tell her this:

"The animal lover population is already the smallest. We cannot afford to lose you. There are countless animals waiting for homes, and the number of people who want those animals is growing very slowly. If we don't adopt animals because losing them is too hard, then the number of people who want them is only going to shrink. That is too sad."

Again, this is a switch of focus from *you* to **them**. Instead of dwelling on how painful it is for us to lose a dog, think this way: *Since the day **he** was rescued, **he** was well-loved and protected. **His** life was rewritten. **He** lived a kick-ass life.* That's enough, my friend.

I want to share a story with you.

There was this young kitten at the shelter, and he was skittish and scared, which put him in a very unfavorable position for adoption. After all, everybody wants an affectionate and cuddly cat. Who wants to adopt a cat that hisses at you? The shelter was always overloaded, so socializing with these types of kitties to make them more adoptable was just not possible for us. A few months went by, the kittens grew fast, and he soon grew into a quiet boy who was invisible when adopters walked by.

Living in the shelter with so many other cats is extremely stressful for them. Day by day, this kitty was looking a little paler and weaker. Because I had seen it many times before, I knew he was dying.

To my surprise, I found this brave couple, Madia and Brandon, who were willing to take him home. They wanted him to experience love, for once in his life, and to finish the journey with him. They named him Odin. I remember that afternoon, my tears were just uncontrollable while I was quietly packing a little bag for Odin. I kissed him farewell and put him into a small carrier. It was the best-looking one I could find in the shelter, though still a little rundown. I had him on one side of my shoulder as I anxiously waited at the back door for his new family to arrive. We were located in the middle of nowhere, and I didn't know that this kind-hearted couple didn't even have a car. I saw a taxi bumping towards me down the sandy, rocky road. Brandon, a really tall, big man, got out. We immediately hugged, and he said, "Maggie, you have a big heart."

I can't thank them enough for what they did for little Odin.

A few days later, they messaged me that Odin had passed away. They described to me every detail of how they were with him, full of love, to the very end. I was sitting in my kitchen, and I told them how much I was crying as we texted. They were crying too. But we all agreed that they were happy tears and that we were smiling inside of our hearts.

When it comes to the day our animals leave us, devastating as it may be, instead of mourning with a heart full of sorrow, I want all the foster parents and adopters to smile with happy tears.

And guess what? There is an antidote. One way to help heal your loss is to bring home another rescued animal that needs you! You have no idea how golden you are. You are a good parent, and you have experience. Don't let that go to waste! Wipe your tears, and get ready to pour your love into another lucky animal! Your heart will be filled immediately. When I say immediately, I mean immediately. You can count on it.

Little Odin on the right.

His little friend on the left, even more skittish, also passed away at the shelter due to sickness.

PART V

MY ROAD

The Unfolding

To wrap up my story, this was how I shared this way of thinking with my company for the last four years. I only had ONE purpose: to persuade my company to stay away from animal entertainment.

My boss is a seventy-year-old traditional Korean man who had never been exposed to my perspective on animals. One hundred percent of what I was trying to say about the animals was completely new and foreign to him. On top of that, he can only understand 50% of my broken Korean.

But I am beyond thankful that he hears me.

Of course, it wasn't easy, and I cannot count how many times I was so frustrated, fed up, and disappointed, but there wasn't a single time it ever crossed my mind to quit.

I'm happy to say that my proposal for a farm animal sanctuary has received the company's full support and has been officially incorporated into this nature park project.*

It may sound like my mission has been accomplished, but far from it. Like any investment project, there are a gazillion unknowns and uncertainties. I am only a tiny cog in the big machine. I have no idea what the future holds, or if I will ever witness the creation of this nature park or animal sanctuary. However, I am very grateful that throughout the process, I've had opportunities to influence others to change their way of thinking about animals. These people, like my boss, have major influence on other business owners, investors, and professionals.

At the end of the day, it's the journey and the impact that matter most, and I continue to learn to live and embrace the present moment as it unfolds.

---

* To clarify, this project is not solely about the sanctuary. The whole project itself is a forest nature theme park consisting of various components such as resorts, glamping, activities, shops, and restaurants, with the farm animal sanctuary being one small part of the park.

To All the Animal Lovers,

I do not expect this book to change you overnight. When I first presented these three questions to my company, although they immediately knew they agreed with my position, it still took close to a year for them to slowly accept it, another year to transition, and yet another year to become supportive.

It might also take you years to accept, to adjust, and, one day, to finally walk away from animal entertainment, and that's okay. I have faith in you.

Just promise me this: if that moment ever arrives and you're ready to embark on this journey with me, reach out and share it. For that is the very purpose behind this book! I'll be here, celebrating the change, jumping with joy, and, together, we'll make this journey feel less lonely.

Keep Dreaming,
Keep Chasing

As for me, I am extremely thankful for having found my dream. Many people have said to me, "If I could afford it, I'd love to do what you do." You might think that I must have a rich husband, allowing me to spend so much time at the shelter and to "pursue my dream." The embarrassing secret is I was never able to afford it. It's a long story, but during those years, we were caught in the perfect storm, and all I can say is that if you earned a minimum wage, you were far wealthier than us.

But the experience taught me something astonishing: *how to give the most when I had the least, and how to be the most generous when I was at my poorest.* When I was going through the toughest years in my life, when I thought I had lost just about everything, it was this dream that kept me alive.

Although I never doubt that I am walking in the right direction, I still often feel lost, unable to see what lies in front of me. Especially since dreams and money are never friends, I sometimes feel very defeated wondering how much longer I have to endure, how many more years I have to eat instant noodles for dinner.

There was a time when my mom was quite proud of me. For once, she thought her daughter was finally independent, making good money, and had a bright future ahead. In an Asian family, I was lucky she didn't smack me in the face when I tossed all of that away and decided to scoop cat poop every day. She's getting very old now, and I feel useless whenever I think about whether I will ever be able to show her that I'm not just a cat maniac and make sure she does not worry about me anymore.

But because I cannot see every step ahead on this road, that's what makes this trip *super* exciting. All I can do is walk one little step every day. I don't know what lies ahead. It might be bright at the end of the tunnel or it might be hard for a while.

But one thing I know for sure: Animals bring out

the kindest side of me. When I'm working with animals, that's when I feel most alive. When I'm presenting or talking to people about animals, I literally feel my body shooting out beams of energy, and it makes me want to "shoot" everyone.

Though this road is rough, I am very willing to walk it. Because when I keep dreaming, I can live my life with passion and energy to keep chasing.

PART VI

CONCLUSION

Be Curious, Be Skeptical

My message in this book is very simple.

First, every time you see a place that has animals, ask yourself these three questions:

1. Where are the animals from?

2. Why are the animals here?

3. Where will the animals go?

These three questions will work for ALL scenarios, and the answers will determine whether you should support or ditch that place.

Don't feel defeated. Give yourself time to adjust, but it's important that you keep repeating these three questions to assess each place with animals you visit.

At some point, I think you will want to walk away from animal entertainment.

Second, watch out for FAKE sanctuaries.

Be curious, be skeptical, ask questions, and only support true sanctuaries. Don't let the disguises fool you.

Finally, here's the real kicker about animal entertainment — it's not just about how animals are treated. The most upsetting part is that the animal entertainment industry tricks us into believing we are "animal lovers," but this is not true! We are supporting businesses that exploit us and harm animals for their own profit. It's time for everyone to be aware of this. As humanity, we should not tolerate such deception.

From the bottom of my heart, thank you for letting me speak to you by reading this book to the end. Congratulations on taking a big step towards a kinder world for animals!

PART VII

FREQUENTLY
ASKED QUESTIONS

More Questions?

You probably have questions still swirling in your mind. In this section, I'll address some deeper questions that emerge from this discussion. However, I will stay focused on animal entertainment in this book, so I won't be covering other topics such as veganism.

But My Kids Love Zoos...

If we want to see animals, we should go to where they live and where they belong. Instead, we capture them and bring them to where we live, where they don't belong.

If you are a parent, you must be shaking your head. *Yeah right, so my kids want to see lions and elephants, and you're suggesting I buy plane tickets and pay for the whole family to go on a safari in Africa?*

It may sound ridiculous to you.

But think about the lions and elephants! They are such incredibly huge creatures that are meant to run free in the wild. When we capture them, load them onto a plane or a ship, and put them into a glass enclosure, why don't we feel ridiculous?

You might think it's easier for me to make this argument because I got to visit the zoo when I was a kid. I saw lots of animals, and I even watched the dolphin show. That ONE DAY was really fun, until I found out it cost the animals their ENTIRE LIVES.

Let me repeat: my one day of fun came at the expense of the animals' entire lives! Trust me, these realizations have kept slapping me in the face throughout the writing of this book, and now I can barely feel my cheeks as they flush with shame.

I don't think it would have made any difference in my childhood if I had not gone to the zoo that one day of the year. But those few visits definitely have a shocking impact on my life now when I realize what it cost.

You might think your children would feel upset and left out if they have to say no while all their friends are going to the zoo. But I have faith this trend is going to flip 180 degrees. Soon, those who still go to the zoo will become the minority.

But only YOU can be the game-changer. Only if we, together, make this effort for our next generation and turn it into a movement, will animal entertainment stop being the norm.

Ask your children how they would feel if they were the animals. Imagine being taken away from your families, taken away from your homes, and shipped to a foreign country where you have to spend your whole life behind glass walls just for other people to look at you.

Educate your children while they're young.

I have never been on a true safari in Africa, and it's on my bucket list. But for the time being, I really enjoy watching animals on YouTube and seeing the native animals that live in my area.

I Wish I Could Just Eat and Sleep All Day!

My sister and I once argued about world-famous zoos and aquariums.

She said these establishments are so wealthy they can provide the best of the best for the animals. The animals don't have to fight or kill to survive, and every meal is designed by nutritionists and served directly to them. They live in temperature-controlled rooms, are cared for by professional handlers, and have vets to tend to their health. All they do is eat, play, and sleep. She wished she could be one of them.

Have you ever had a similar thought?

I'm not surprised if you have.

But it's not that all you do is eat, play, and sleep. It's that all you CAN do is eat, play, and sleep, in that limited enclosure, every day, for the rest of your life.

Do you seriously want to be one of them?

If the animals had a choice, do you think they would choose luxury or freedom?

What If Animals
Could Have Both
Luxury and Freedom?

I 've also had this conversation with businessmen
who had been invited to privately owned zoos in
the Middle East. These zoos were extraordinarily
spacious and impeccably managed. The owners of
the zoos are unimaginably wealthy, and their establishments are not intended for public entertainment.
In these zoos, animals enjoy a lifetime of stress-free
luxury. The owners and visitors to these zoos feel that
the tigers and lions there are living in a paradise, far
better protected than they would be in the wild.

What do you think?

Remember, we can apply the three questions to all scenarios.

1. Where are the animals from? Purchased and bred.

2. Why are the animals here? For the owner's pleasure.

3. Where will the animals go? They will live in the zoo forever.

Hypothetically, even if a zoo has vast amounts of land where the animals can live no differently than in their natural habitat, simply speaking, the owner essentially keeps tigers, lions, and other exotic animals as pets. This concept, as I explained earlier in this book, is at the root of the animal tragedy. The zoo's original intention is to benefit people, not to provide the best for the animals.

So, when we purchase or breed an animal perfectly capable of thriving in the wild and bring them into captivity, even if it's in a luxury zoo, can we truly label it as protection?

I don't think so. Especially when there are so many big cats that already need to be rescued.

Can't Animals Work Too?

My mentor and best friend, who is also an animal lover, challenged me with a very good question:

"Um… I don't quite agree. We humans have to work and sweat to earn a living, so what's wrong with making an animal work?"

Humans have a choice. Animals don't.

Human beings are incredibly intelligent and creative. If they want an animal to do anything, no matter how big or fierce the animal is, they can find ways to make him surrender. Even the fiercest tiger can be intimidated into submission, and the spirit of the largest elephant can be broken to fear the smallest bullhook.

Hundreds of thousands of years ago, people lived a tough life. Animals also lived a tough life. We worked and sweat to meet basic food and living needs, and cows and horses helped us work on farms. But as our lives became richer and more prosperous, we upgraded our wish lists. We began to explore fun and enjoyment, then we started using animals for our entertainment.

If you are not really interested in animal welfare, you might say that there is nothing wrong with animal entertainment. After all, it is an upgraded job too, and is much more comfortable than pulling heavy loads on a farm.

But I want to believe that humanity can be kinder than this.

Instead of always wanting to rule over animals, wouldn't it be better if humanity used our power and creativity to protect those who cannot defend themselves?

Are the Fancy Horseback Riding Lessons Any Different?

I t was incredibly hard for me to tell myself that horseback riding was the same as other forms of animal entertainment. Horseback riding was a core part of my childhood, and I spent many hours at the riding club. I also wanted to convince myself that taking riding lessons was different from going on a one-time trail ride as a tourist or hiring a horse carriage for sightseeing.

I argued with myself:

Horseback riding is a sophisticated sport!

Learning to ride and handle horses is a more in-depth commitment!

These horses are treated way better!

Regardless of how many fancy excuses I tried to find, when I answered the three big questions, I couldn't escape the truth. The horses are being ridden day in and day out, under the hot sun, in the freezing cold, all their lives, until they are old and weak. Many will end their lives in the slaughterhouse or be euthanized, although some will stay with their owners until they die of old age.

I was reluctant to accept this fact because of the time, effort, and money that I put into riding for many years. I took pride in it. *Damn, what do I do with all those awesome pictures of me on a horse? The memories from my youth in the riding club are precious, and I don't want to wipe them out.*

Once again, I realized: I loved myself more than I loved horses.

Riding a horse was fun for me, but what about the horse? It took me years of self-reflection on the entire concept of animal entertainment to come to my decision.

Today, I can confidently tell you that I wish to see horses free to pursue their own lives, wander vast expanses in nature, and play with other horses in large groups, and I don't want to make demands by climbing on top of them.[5]

It is not an impossible life to live. Now I can visit and give my support to horse sanctuaries!

Isn't Keeping Cats Indoors the Same as Life Imprisonment?

Earlier I said that keeping wild animals in a fancy zoo is the equivalent of locking them in a luxury prison. Although they might be well fed and cared for by experts, the space is just too small, and they are deprived of freedom their entire lives.

But when it comes to our cat companions, while many cat parents and vets think that keeping cats indoors is no different from life imprisonment in our homes, I advocate for INDOORS-ONLY living. In fact, this is one of the commitments I require all of my adopters to agree to beforehand.

Why do I have double standards?

Because cats, unfortunately, can no longer be considered wild animals, thanks to humans domesticating them for tens of thousands of years.

Stray cats should not be mistaken for wild cats. Many people call cats that are living on the street "wild" and believe they can do just fine on their own. That is a myth. The reality is, without the help of humans, most cats would live a miserable life.

Now that humans are involved, things get complicated. We must consider the emotional investment and effort we put into our feline companions.

From the standpoint of a rescuer, picking up a distressed-looking cat on the street, caring for her like a mother, transforming her into a brand new kitty, and, in the end, bawling your eyes out when sending her to a new adopter is an emotional rollercoaster.

How would you feel if one day your adopter told you that they let the kitty out and he was run over by a car, or she went missing?

So we keep our kitties indoors to avoid accidents and to protect our own feelings. Aren't we being selfish in that sense?

Yes, in a sense. But this is one case where our selfish feelings align with the cats' needs. All I can say is that the system for cats is already broken. It is irreversible. And we are looking for a remedy, which is imperfect.

Fortunately, there is some comforting news. For those of us who have kitties at home, we know how much they enjoy hanging out by our side, how they won't leave us alone in the bathroom, and that contented, half-drunk expression they have when they purr and knead on our lap. I am convinced that they seem happy because they feel loved.

I am convinced **LOVE is the only compensation** for the already broken system for domesticated cats.

Rescued Cat and Dog Cafés

Obviously, I see animal cafés with kangaroos, alpacas, owls, and other wild animals as a form of animal entertainment. The same goes for cat and dog cafés that involve buying, breeding, and selling cats and dogs.

But in recent years, a new type of café has emerged: cafés for rescued kitties and pups.

Are they good or bad?

At this point, I think I have repeated myself enough. Just ask the three questions.

The animals are all rescued, they are there to find qualified and responsible adopters, and eventually, they will spend the rest of their lives with those adopters living happily ever after.

If the above is true, a rescued cat and dog café is fair game because its purpose is to help rescued animals find homes or provide sanctuary for senior or unadoptable animals. While the café owner might earn a living from this work, that is not the only objective.

How Can an Animal Sanctuary Survive?

Whenever I pitch the concept of an animal sanctuary — whether it's to business people, government officials, or friends — everyone nods to the fantastic idea of providing stress-free environments for animals, not using them for entertainment, and being responsible for their lifelong care. However, without fail, one question pops up: how can an animal sanctuary survive?

Here's my answer: An animal sanctuary can make profits without directly involving the animals. The income comes from entrance fees, food and beverage sales, merchandise, activities, and even lodging facilities. There are plenty of revenue streams to consider.

This usually leaves people scratching their heads. It is because the concept of animal entertainment has grown so deeply into our minds. We pay to bottle-feed a baby cow, we pay to ride a pony, we pay to take pictures with a parrot on our shoulder. We are so used to the business model of animals being direct profit generators. But I'll let you in on a secret: they don't have to be. Think outside the box; there are plenty of ways to be both ethical and profitable.

Am I a Hypocrite for Supporting Farm Animal Sanctuaries While Also Eating Meat?

Y ou might be thinking, *Farm animal sanctuaries rescue farm animals, which are cows, pigs, sheep, goats, and chickens, but I'm not a vegan. I eat all of them. Isn't that weird? I'm confused now!*

Here is my short answer for you:

We cannot be perfect overnight, but we need to be willing to take the first baby step.

Farm animals are considered the most abused creatures on earth as a result of factory farming. We love our cats and dogs to the moon, we care about wild animals going extinct, but we pay little or no attention to farm animals.

As a matter of fact, people who rescue farm animals and start sanctuaries are often vegans, but they love and encourage non-vegan people to visit and get to know more about them. Sanctuaries not only influence animal welfare but also impact the environment and human health. Through visiting a sanctuary, we can learn a lot and be inspired to think more.

Visit as many sanctuaries as you want, as many times as you want. You never know, you may get interested in having a vegan meal once a month, and years later, you may find yourself embracing a vegan lifestyle too!

Meanwhile, I'm sure many of you may say,

"I really enjoy eating meat, so I don't want to know anything about it."

The world never stops changing and improving. We should always strive to become better. Running away and covering our ears to avoid learning the truth is not going to get us anywhere. So don't be afraid to know more and learn more.

We cannot be perfect, and we cannot change overnight. While we are far from perfect or even far from good, don't be afraid to take one step forward and give a tiny thought to farm animals. Collectively, our individual efforts to change, no matter how small, can have a huge impact on these animals' lives.

About the Author

Maggie Cheung (originally Lok Ha Cheung) describes herself as a nobody who just loves cats. After adopting her first cat, she realized there were so many stray cats and that humans were responsible for creating the situation in the first place. Later, she quit her job in the financial sector to dedicate her life to cat rescues and the grassroots movement to switch from animal entertainment to animal sanctuaries.

Acknowledgments

Thank you to Joanne Lefson at Farm Sanctuary SA (Franschhoek, South Africa), Ashley Pankratz at Farm Sanctuary (Watkins Glen, New York, USA), and Nicky Vernon at Greyton Farm Animal Sanctuary (Greyton, South Africa) for your kindness and generosity in giving attention and so much help to a random person who just started writing to you.

When I first started crafting this animal sanctuary idea, I didn't know a single thing about where to start or what to do. I reached out to a few organizations, wrote them a fairly long letter, and then closed my hands and prayed. When I heard that "ding" from my email, I ran to my phone, my heart pounding, opened my inbox, and cried, "YES!" Your response meant the world to me.

You might think you didn't do much, but just pointing me in the right direction has meant a great deal to me. I understand we live in a world with busy schedules and skepticism. The fact that you were willing to give me your time and patience is something I will never take for granted.

Most importantly, I believe your kindness and generosity come from your passion and love for animals, and that gives me so many sparks of joy and strength to continue. I would not have come this far without your help. Thank you!

I would also like to express my deepest and heart-felt thanks to Rick Warren for his transformative book *The Purpose Driven Life*, which revolutionized my perspective on life's meaning. The very first line of the book reads, "It's not about you." He means, our life is not about us. That hit me like an arrow!

That was the first time I acknowledged living a self-centered existence, where everything revolved around me, everything was about me and myself only. No wonder I felt lost and empty about my existence. Warren says we are not put in this world to merely take up space, consume resources, and just keep wanting more. Everyone is created by God with a purpose — **to give** and **to be used**.

While the concept of giving is beautiful, being used may sound harsh and exploitative. But consider this: Objects like a pen, a phone, or a cooking pot are created with a simple purpose — to be used. Humans, on the other hand, are gifted with love and free will, but we often overlook that we are also created "to be used" to serve a purpose. Embracing the idea that "Our life is not about us" challenges us to think less about ourselves and be more useful to others.

My life was never the same again.

Warren's book turned me from a skeptical non-believer to someone who is dedicating their life to be used by God. Had it been the old version of me, I would not have had the slightest courage to embark on my current journey. My life has since become simpler, easier, and clearer. Though I'm starting from scratch, everything I'm learning to do now — to love, to give, and to be used — I do it with a passion, knowing this is the purpose of my life.

Notes

[1] "How to Get a Cow Pregnant." *GROW Magazine*, October 23, 2008. https://grow.cals.wisc.edu/deprecated/agriculture/how-to-get-a-cow-pregnant.

[2] Levitt, Tom. "The End of Dairy's 'Dirty Secret'? Farms Have a Year to Stop Killing Male Calves." *The Guardian*, December 14, 2020. https://www.theguardian.com/environment/2020/dec/10/the-end-of-dairys-dirty-secret-farms-have-a-year-to-stop-killing-male-calves.

[3] Hall, Jani. "Exotic Pet Trade, Explained." *National Geographic*, February 21, 2019. https://www.nationalgeographic.com/animals/article/exotic-pet-trade.

[4] Jae-Hee, Choi. "Horse's Death after Cruel TV Stunt Is in Spotlight. But Life Is No Better for Other Ex-Racehorses." *The Korea Herald*, January 24, 2022. https://www.koreaherald.com/view.php?ud=20220124000742.

[5] PETA. "How Does PETA Feel About Horseback Riding?" December 1, 2017. https://www.peta.org/about-peta/faq/how-does-peta-feel-about-horseback-riding.

Bibliography

Griffler, Mckenzee. "Why Residents Shouldn't Breed At A Farmed Animal Sanctuary." The Open Sanctuary Project, April 2, 2019. https://opensanctuary.org/why-a-farmed-animal-sanctuary-shouldnt-breed-residents/.

PETA. "How to Tell If a Place Is a REAL Animal Sanctuary." November 30, 2022. https://www.peta.org/features/real-animal-sanctuary-zoo.

PETA Exposes and Undercover Investigations. "K-Cruelty: South Korea's Horse-Slaughter Industry." July 20, 2021. https://investigations.peta.org/south-korea-horse-slaughter/.

Warren, Rick. *The Purpose Driven Life*. Zondervan, 2007.

Printed in Great Britain
by Amazon